A Mark Dahle Portfolio

Lat's Collapse

Present Divestment #4

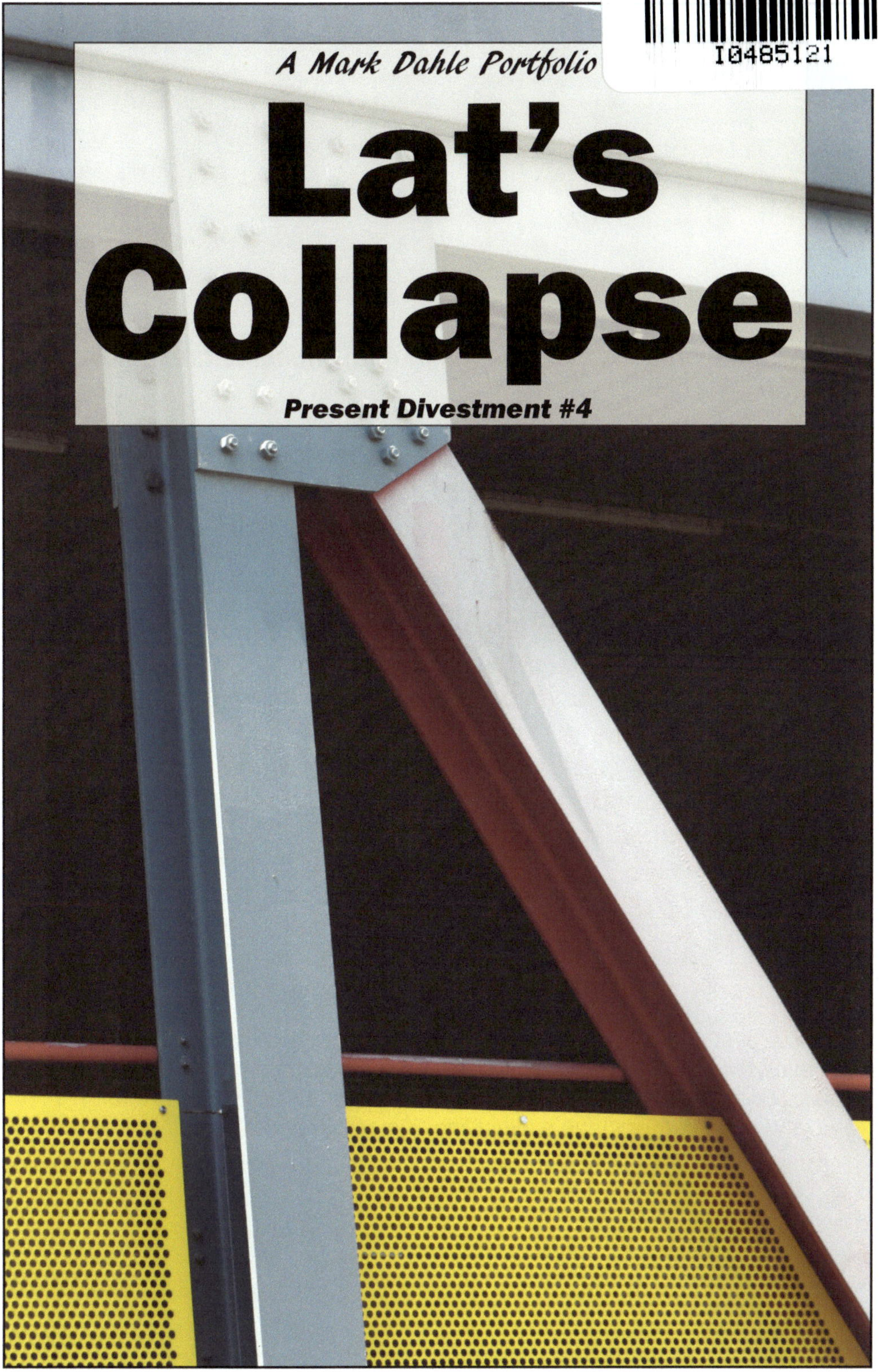

Mark Dahle Portfolios can be read in a few minutes and enjoyed for a lifetime.

This portfolio includes the fourth story in the Present Divestment series, a photo of a beautiful 36 x 24 inch painting (at the right) and twenty-five outstanding photographs from Basel, Switzerland.

Unlike many picture books, the text is unrelated to the paintings and photographs. This might seem weird at first. One thing that helps is to order more portfolios until you get used to it.

Photographs in this book are available in limited editions. See http://www.MarkDahle.com for more information and for previews of upcoming portfolios.

We do our best to create portfolios free of editing mistakes. But it's hard to catch everything. We reward people who report errors in any Mark Dahle portfolio. For details see MarkDahle.com/Typos.html or send an email to MarkDahle@aol.com with the subject line "Typos." Thanks!

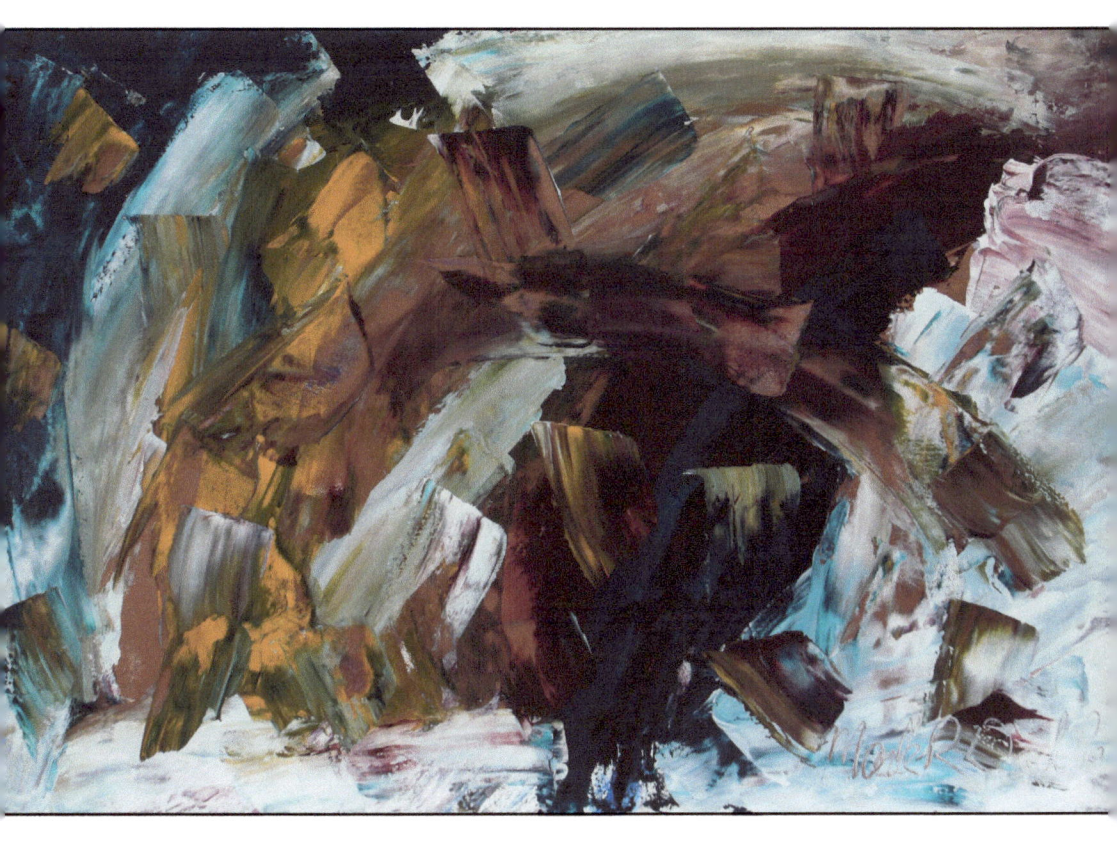

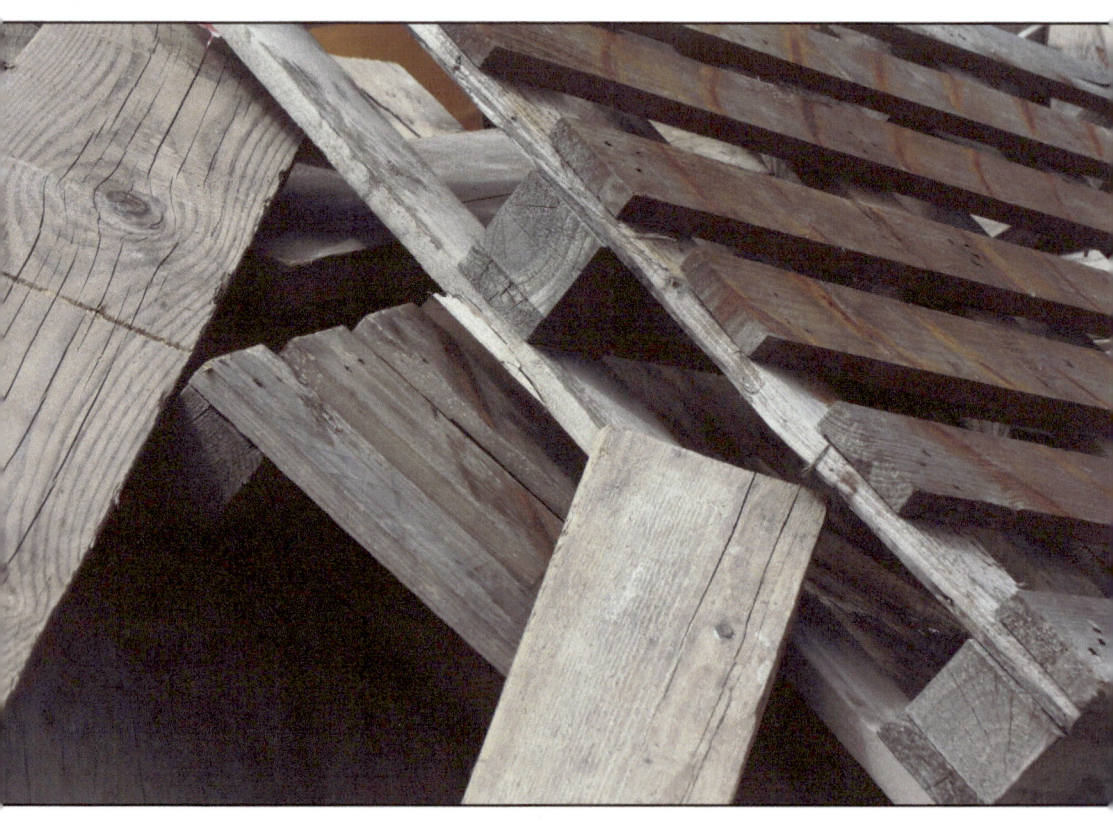

J-rex watched on monitors as the second doors of the Decontamination Chamber slowly slid open. Even when they were just inches apart, Lat could see and hear the mayhem. He watched in stunned silence as the doors opened, revealing the extent of the damage. Fifteen minutes before, the room had been sterile and clean. Now there was broken glass everywhere, smashed equipment, small fires, electric sparks showering from slashed wires, smoke, and, he finally saw, movement – a gator racing the length of the room straight towards Lat, moving as fast as it could go.

Lat hastily pushed the button to secure the door. But the door was designed to create a complete seal, not to move quickly, and the gator arrived long before the door could shut.

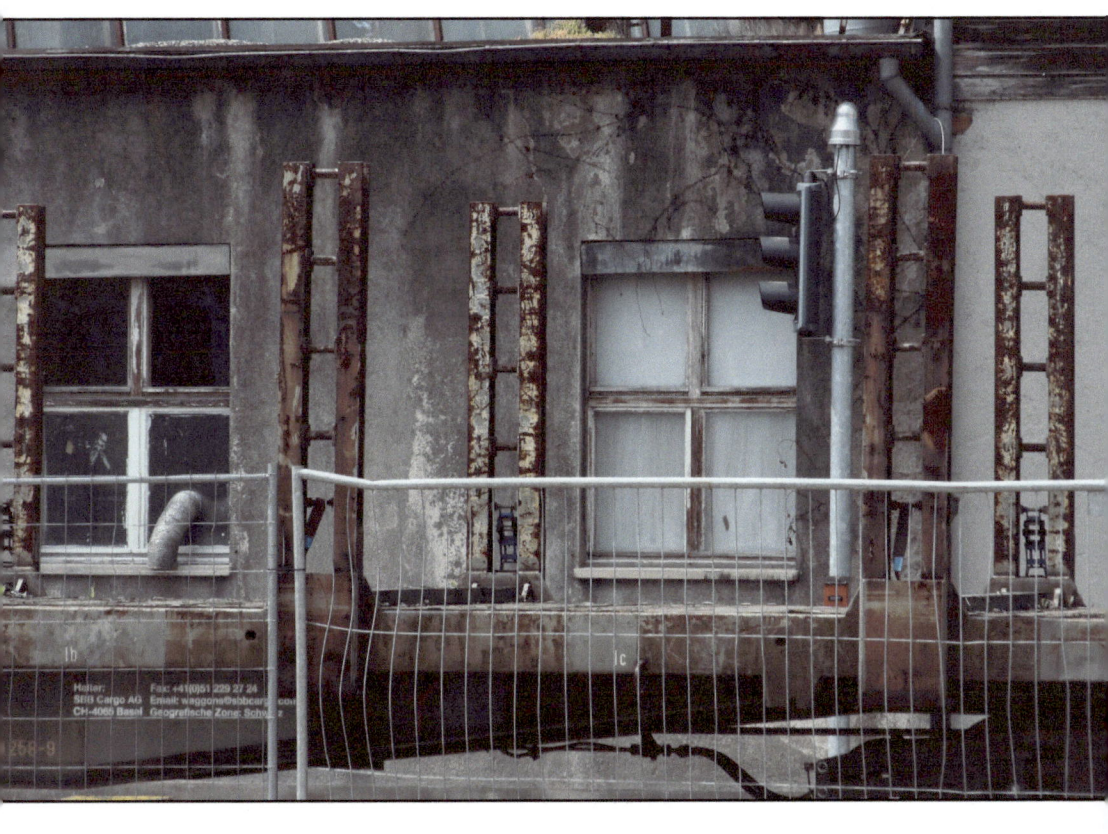

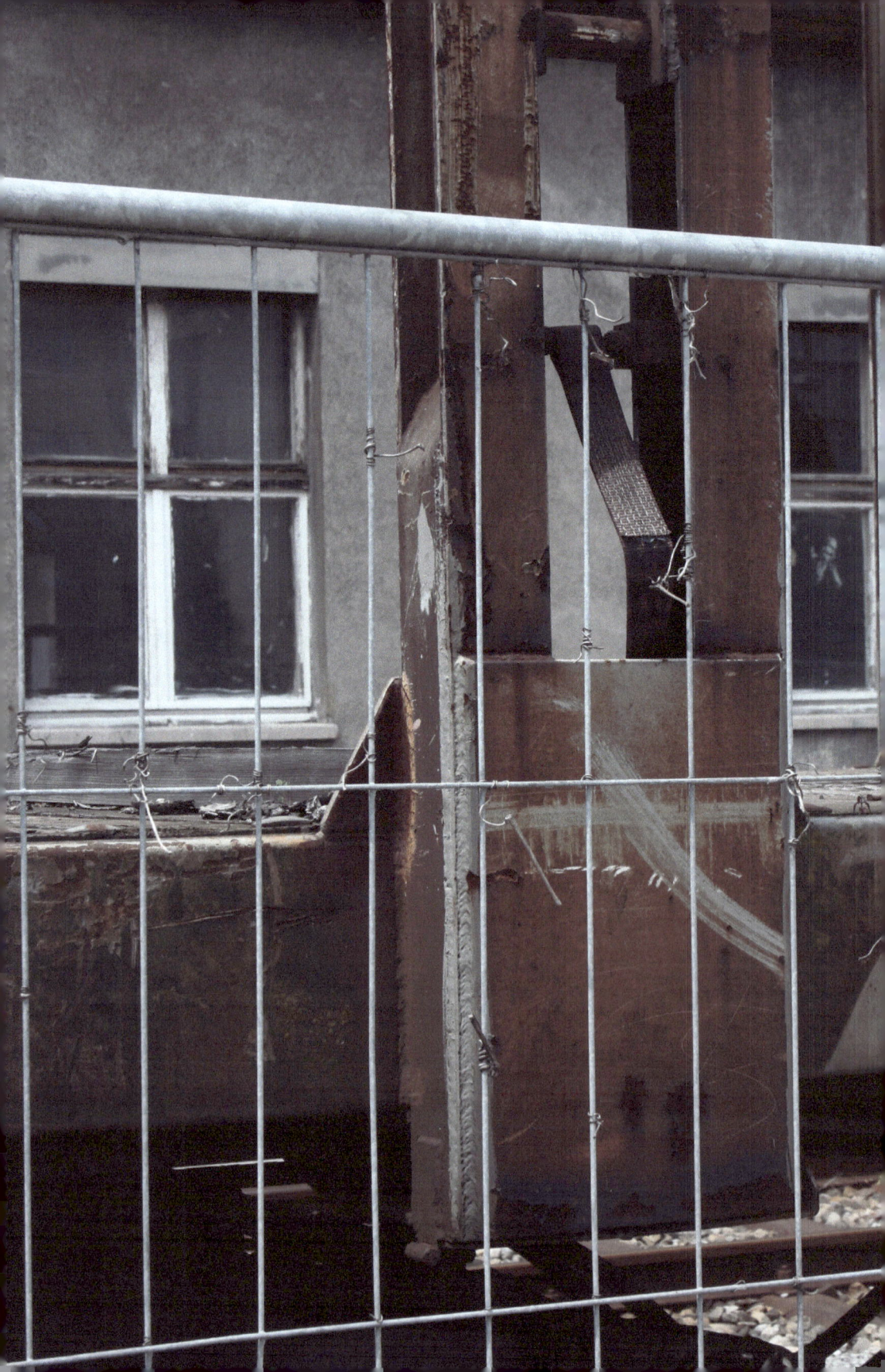

Given the mayhem in the room, J-rex thought the gator would kill Lat in a split-second. To his surprise, the gator raced straight towards Lat and stopped, inches away. It didn't attack. Instead, the life seemed to leave it. The gator sank to the ground, like a balloon deflating. But Lat, who had not even been scratched, suddenly looked like he was fighting for his life. His face convulsed, then his body. He writhed and contorted, then straightened, looked like he had returned to normal – and collapsed into the main room, just outside the Decontamination Chamber doors, quite close to a sparking electric wire.

The gator suddenly came back to life. It slithered around Lat and went into the Decontamination Chamber, hitting Lat further into the main room with its tail, pushing him closer to one of the burning fires.

When the gator reached the back of the Decontamination Chamber, it tested the strength of the exit doors.

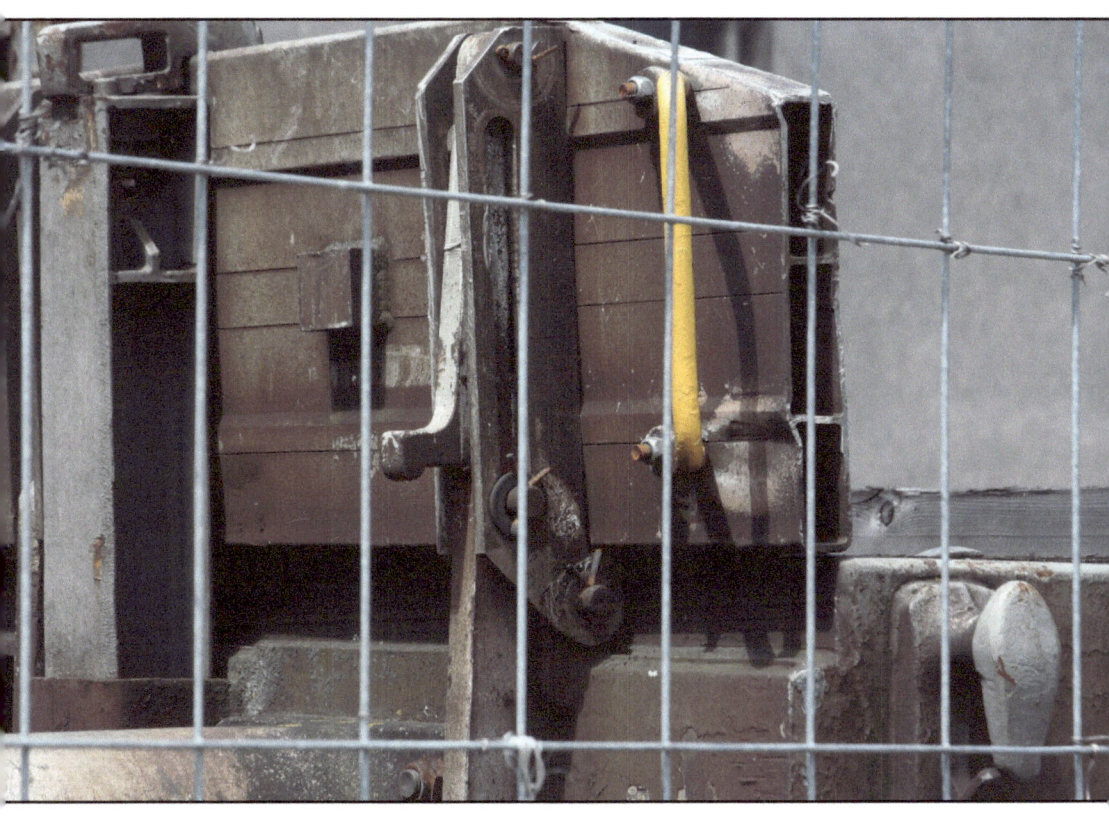

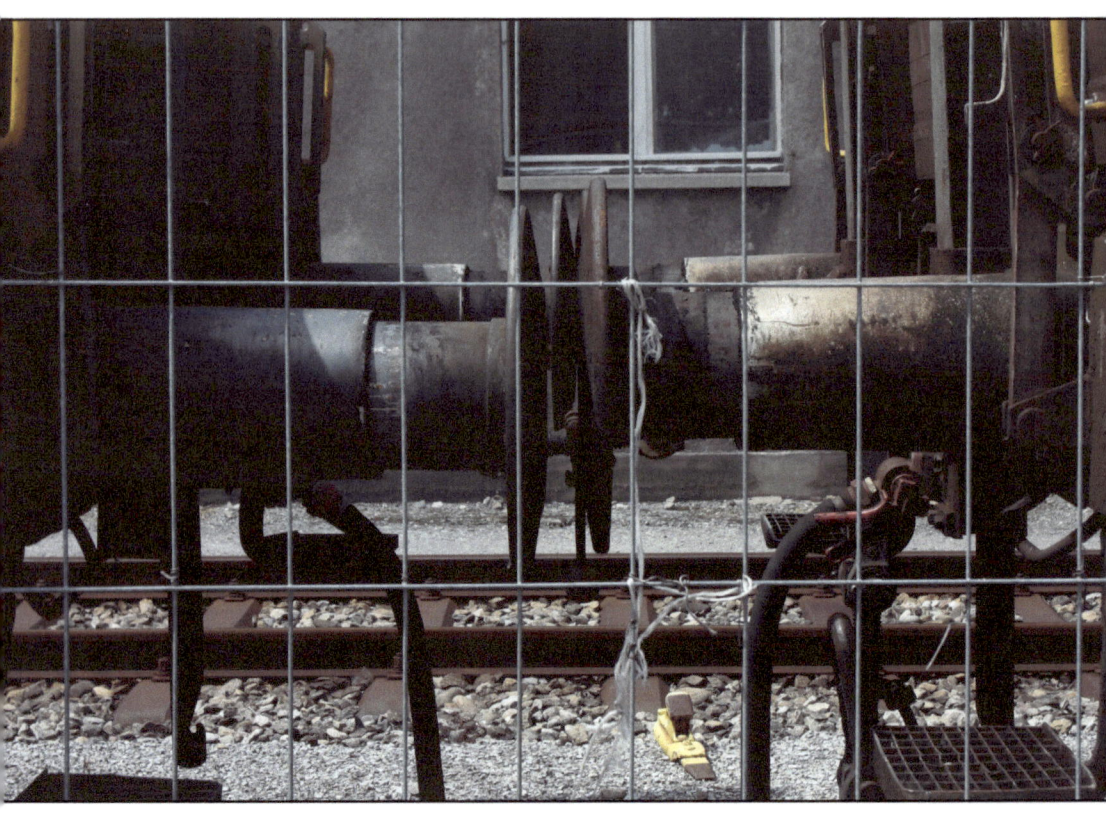

For a half-minute, Lat was unconscious, dreaming. In his dream he heard the terrifying sound of a furious slithering as an alligator rushed straight towards him. Fear was making it hard to breathe. He was almost suffocated with it. Then he coughed and woke up.

At first it was hard to realize what he was looking at was not still the dream. The launch site was in shambles. Lat was cut from some of the glass. He had coughed because smoke from the fires was making it hard to breathe.

Lat rose unsteadily, keeping his body close to the floor and the remaining oxygen. He could hardly control his movement. All his joints were in pain and he was shaking. But his memory returned with a start, and he quickly reached over and hit the button shutting the door to the Decontamination Chamber. The gator, still trying to smash its way out the other end, was trapped inside, for now.

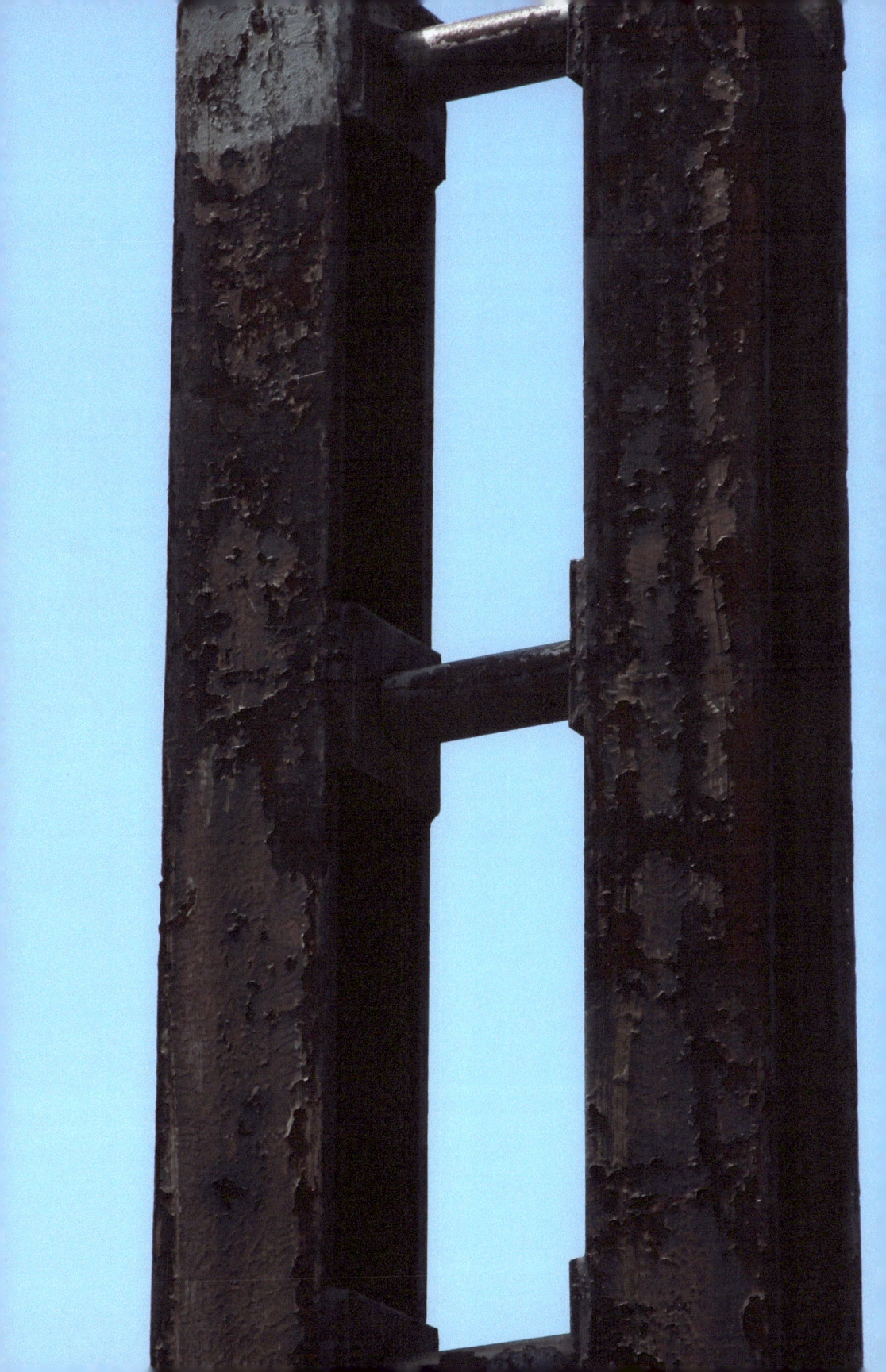

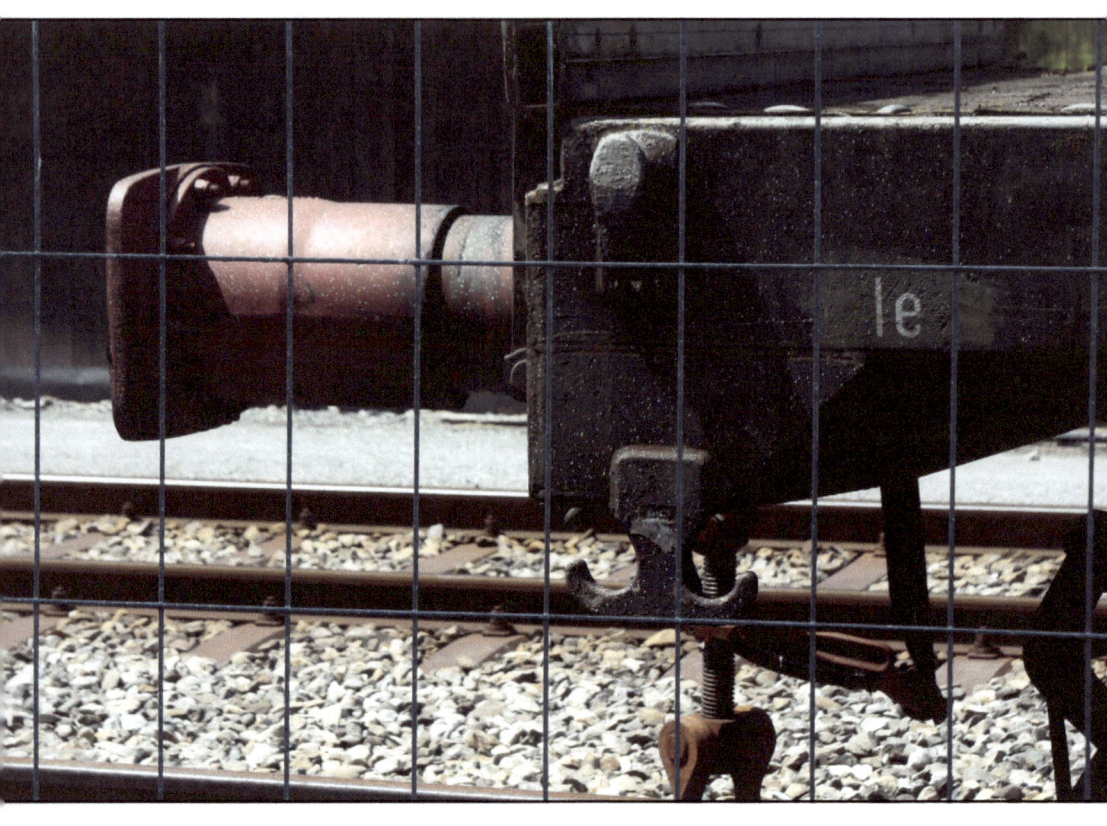

Lat put a cloth to his face so he could breathe easier and grabbed a fire extinguisher. The first blaze was fairly easy to put out. The second was harder. Lat finally reduced it to a smoldering pile of charcoal and melted plastic. The third fire, however, had almost reached the point where it couldn't be stopped. Lat emptied three fire extinguishers on it before he got the blaze under control.

Next Lat turned on the exhaust fan, glad that it still worked, and sat on the ground, coughing, in the center of the destruction. The thick chemical smell from the fire extinguishers was almost worse than the smoke. But the air began clearing as soon as he turned on the fan, and Lat sat on the ground until the air was good enough for him to stand.

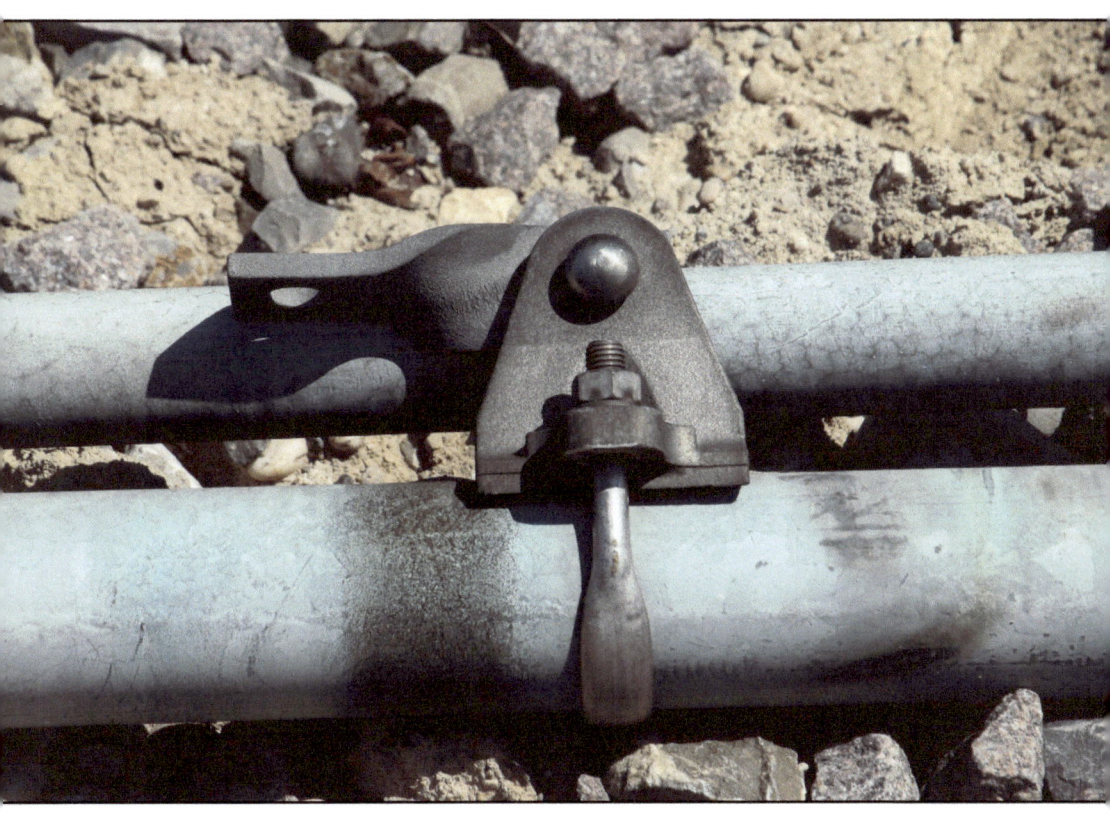

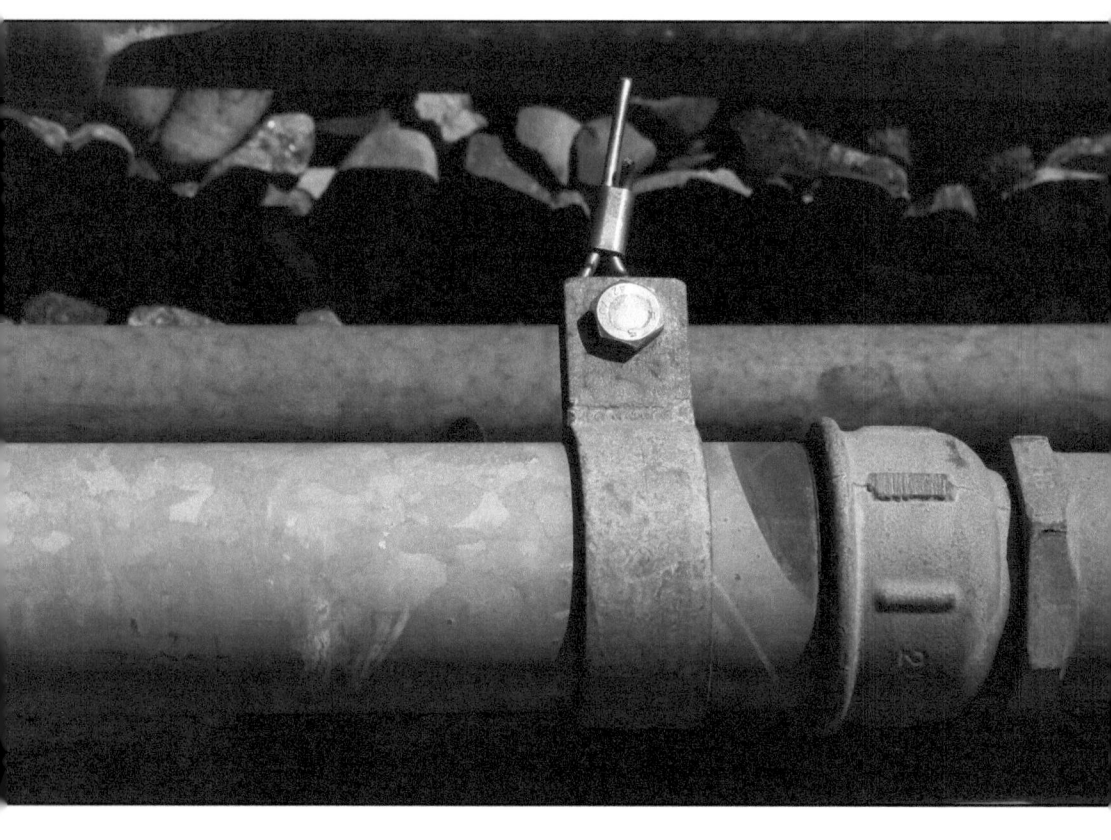

The SecurPhone rang on J-rex's desk. Lat had clearance for almost everything in the room. The phone, however, was reserved for J-rex alone. But at this point Lat guessed it didn't matter.

"This is Lat," he said, picking it up.

"Lat, I'm glad you survived." J-rex said. "The InfoCom is down, so this phone is our only link until we get things fixed. How are you feeling?"

"My lungs hurt so bad I can hardly stand it. My whole body feels beat up. But I'm okay."

"Is there anyone else in the launch site?"

"Anyone else?"

The thought hadn't occurred to Lat. He'd been so focused on the gator and the immediate problems, he hadn't started to think about ways that things might be worse than they appeared.

"Make a clean sweep," J-rex said. "I want to confirm that the gator actually did all that damage."

"Where did the gator *come* from?" Lat asked.

"I'm reviewing surveillance video right now. At the moment, I've gotten to where the gator was opened up in the autopsy and then stitched back up."

It took a moment for Lat to realize what J-rex meant.

"You think the gator in the Decompression Chamber is the dead gator we've been examining for three days? There's zero chance of that."

"Just check the room. I'll keep watching the video."

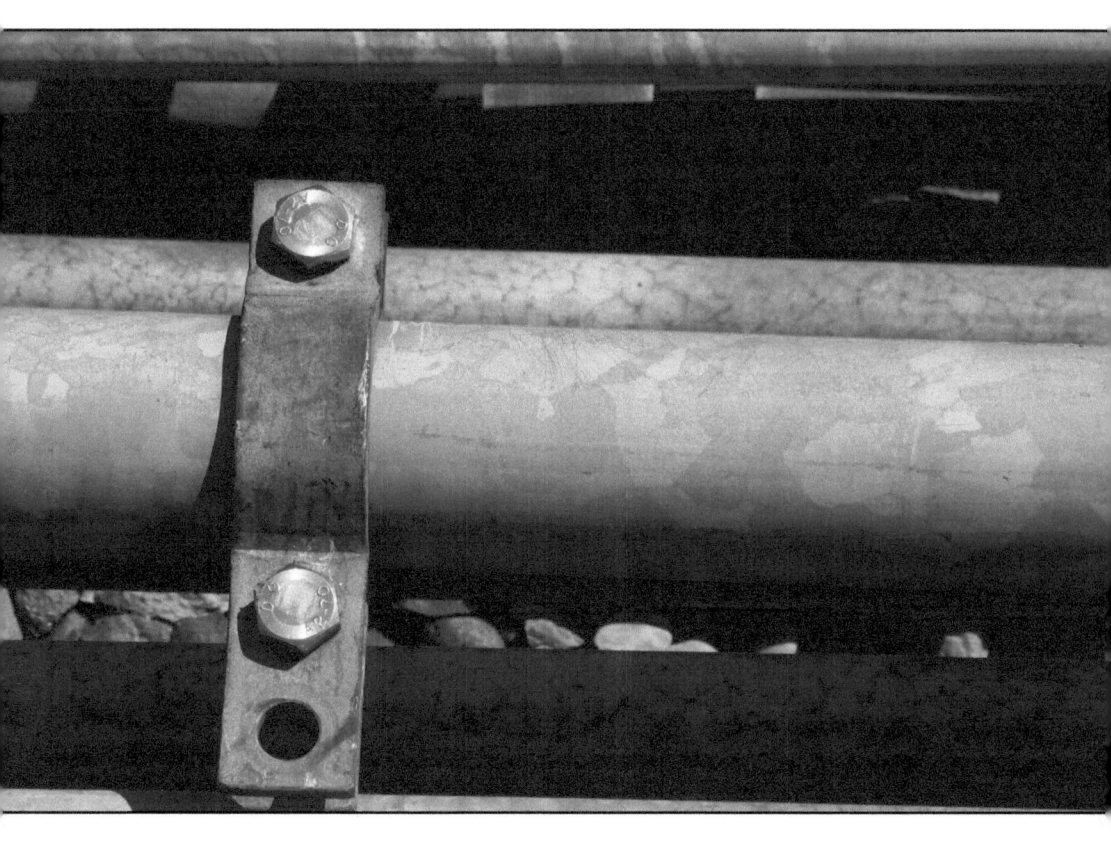

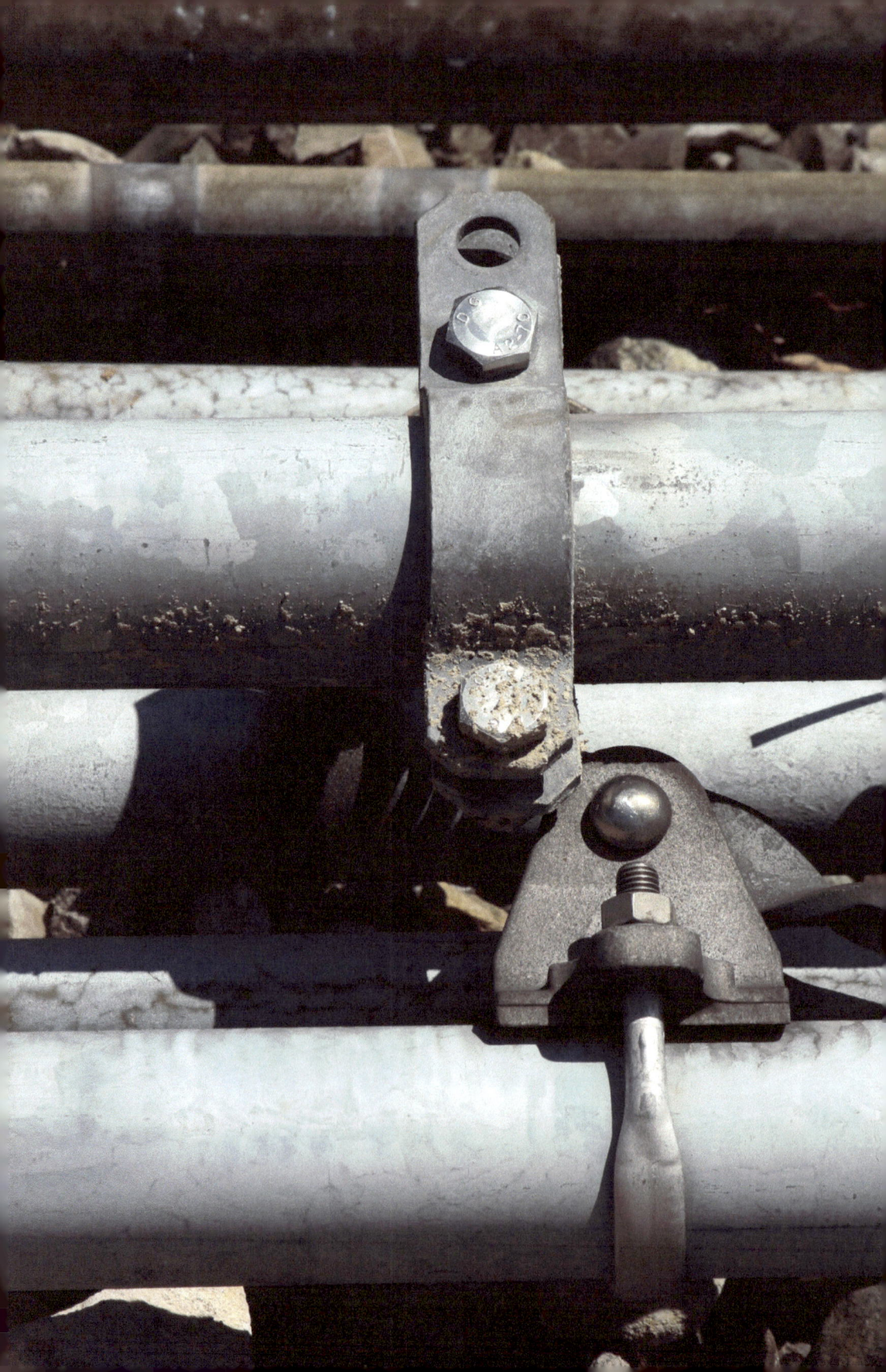

Lat opened every drawer, every file cabinet, and every hiding place in the room, expecting to find something hideous each time he pulled a door open. But the room was as empty as he had left it, just the same except for massive damage everywhere he looked.

As Lat checked the room, he told J-rex what needed to be replaced. It was a long list.

The biggest loss was Transporter One. Lat guessed it was beyond repair. The machine was so delicate, if you replaced only what *looked* broken, how you could trust the rest of the parts to all still work? But building another Transporter could take a year.

"It won't take a year," said J-rex. "We've been working on a new prototype. It'll be ready soon enough. But it's still in the testing phase."

Lat grimaced. With this much damage, he knew the Corporation wouldn't be willing to wait for the tests to be complete. It was likely Se would be sent to the future before everything was ready on the prototype.

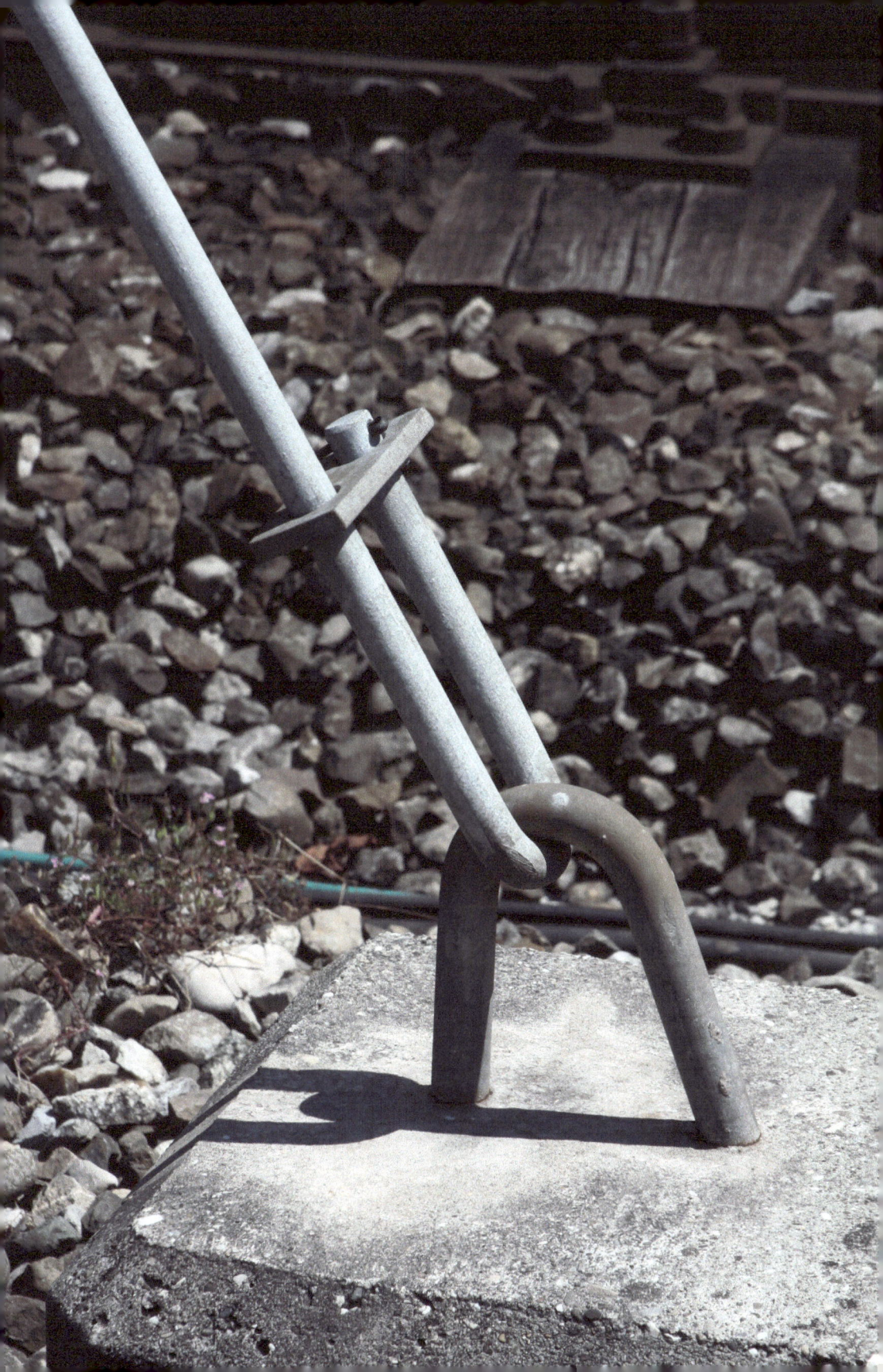

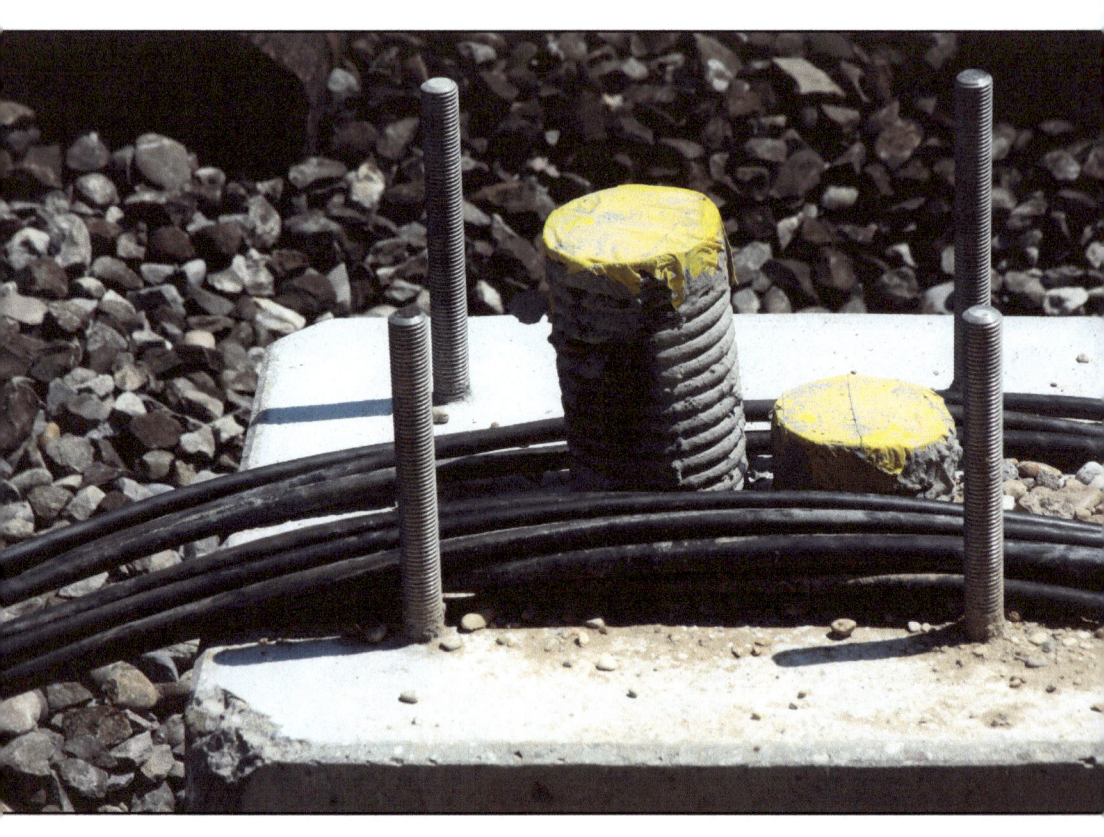

Lat examined the DeepFreeze where the autopsied gator had been stored. The door had been forced open. Its hinges were sprung, and now it wouldn't fully close. There was no gator inside.

Lat still didn't want to believe that J-rex could be right – that what had created all the damage was the same gator as the one the team had thought was dead for so long. How could they not have detected any signs of life over three days? Why hadn't anything shown up on the medical probes? It didn't make sense.

Lat searched all the rooms top to bottom twice before he was satisfied that there was no one else in the space.

"If that lively gator and our dead gator are the same, you'd better go to ten or eleven," Lat said. "I'd like to call Lara first, if you think there's time."

Lat knew that even at ten, the plant he was in would be destroyed. He was just hoping it would take out the gator, too. But this gator? Maybe even their protocols wouldn't help.

"I suggested level ten before you arrived," J-rex said. "The Director refused. He said he wouldn't go past nine."

"Nine? Is he out of his mind?"

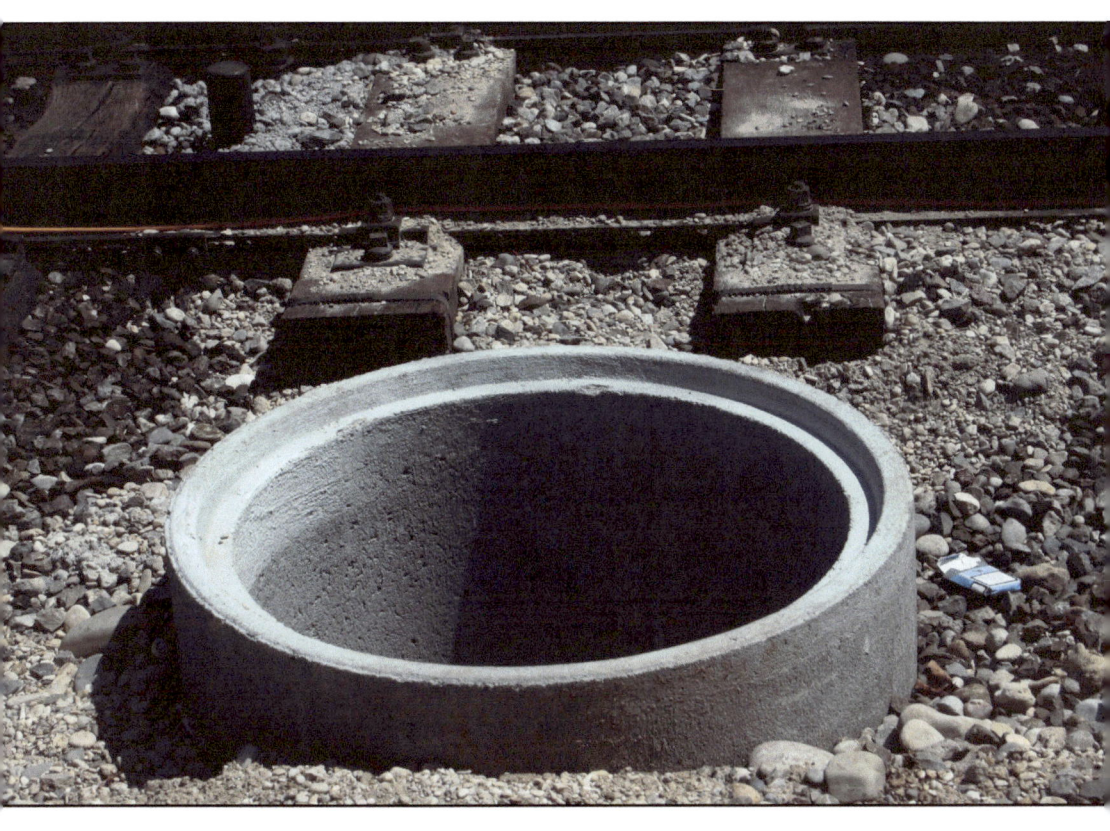

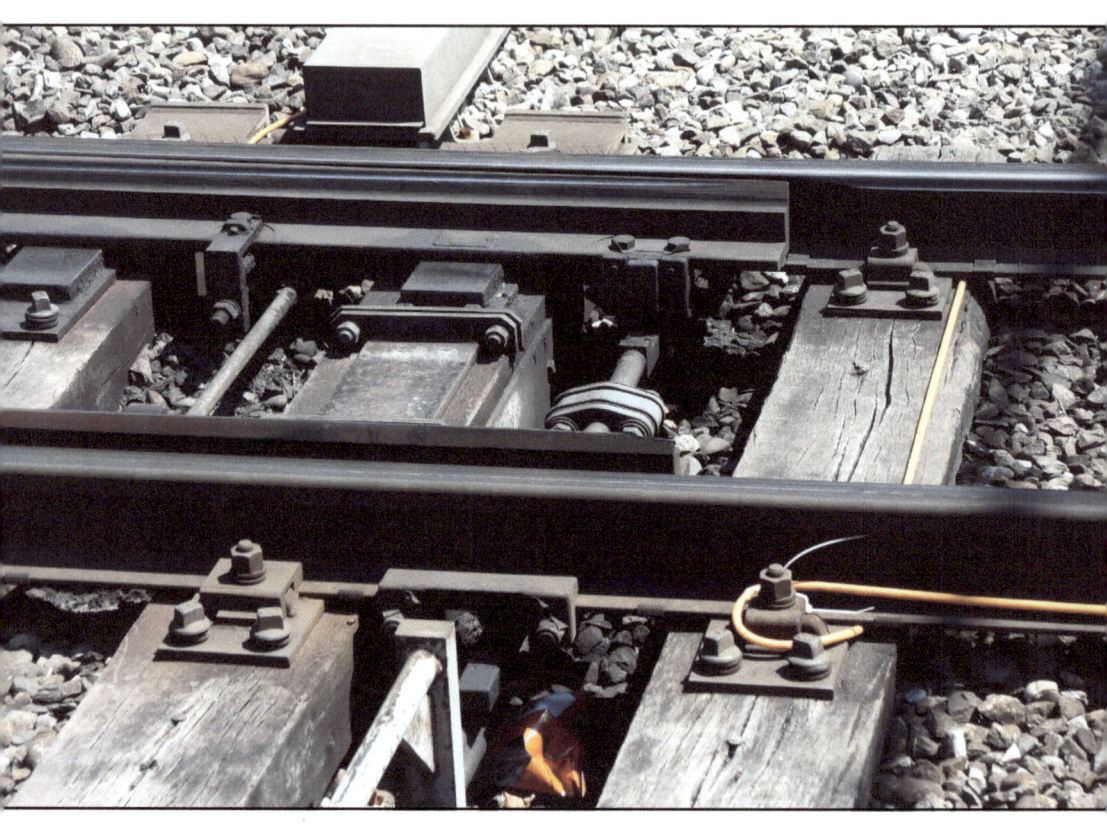

"He hasn't seen what you've seen. But it's worse than that. He's moving slowly. Right now we're just at seven."

"SEVEN? There's only two sets of doors between that thing and the main building. And if it can get out of the Decontamination Chamber, it won't have any trouble busting out of the entrance doors."

"I know. I've got three SecurPatrol teams on their way."

Lat frowned. He doubted the SecurPatrols would have the right weapons for a dead gator that could behave like this one.

The mention of extra teams reminded Lat why he had headed back to the launch site.

His own monitor and desk were smashed, but Paul's was untouched. He logged onto Paul's machine and pulled up the records of the teams that had left on break only a half hour before.

He whistled.

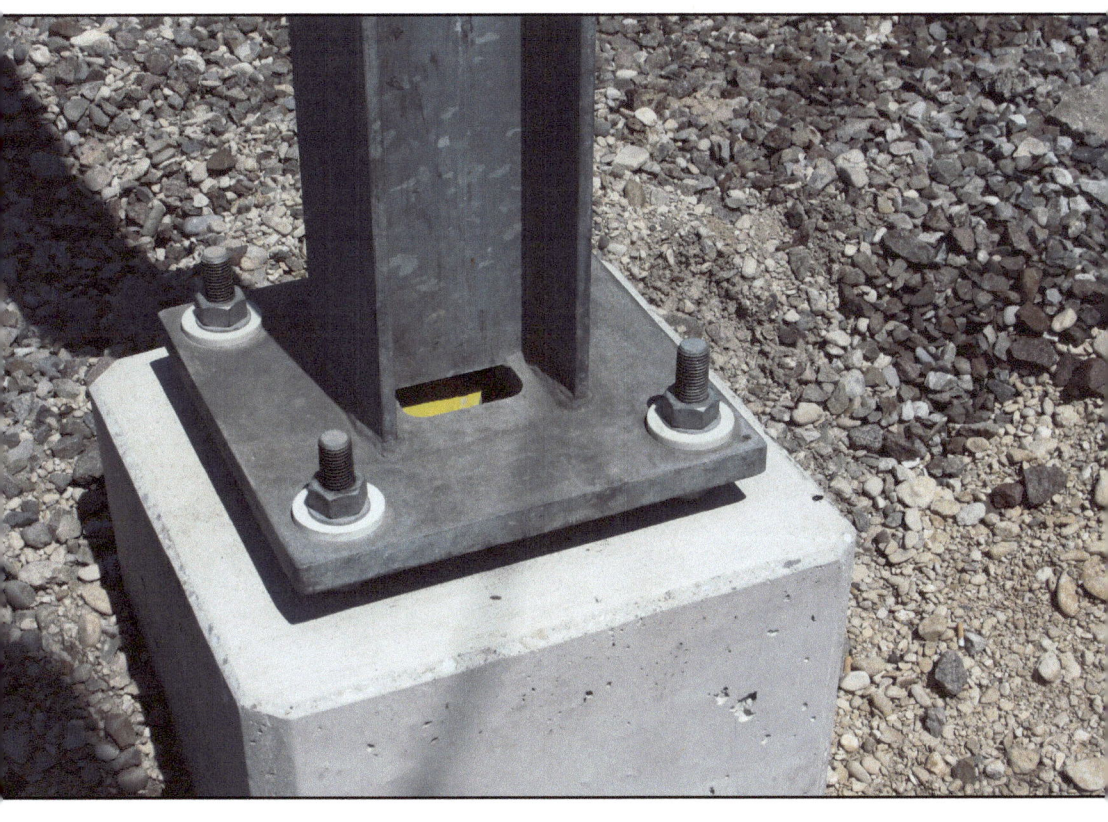

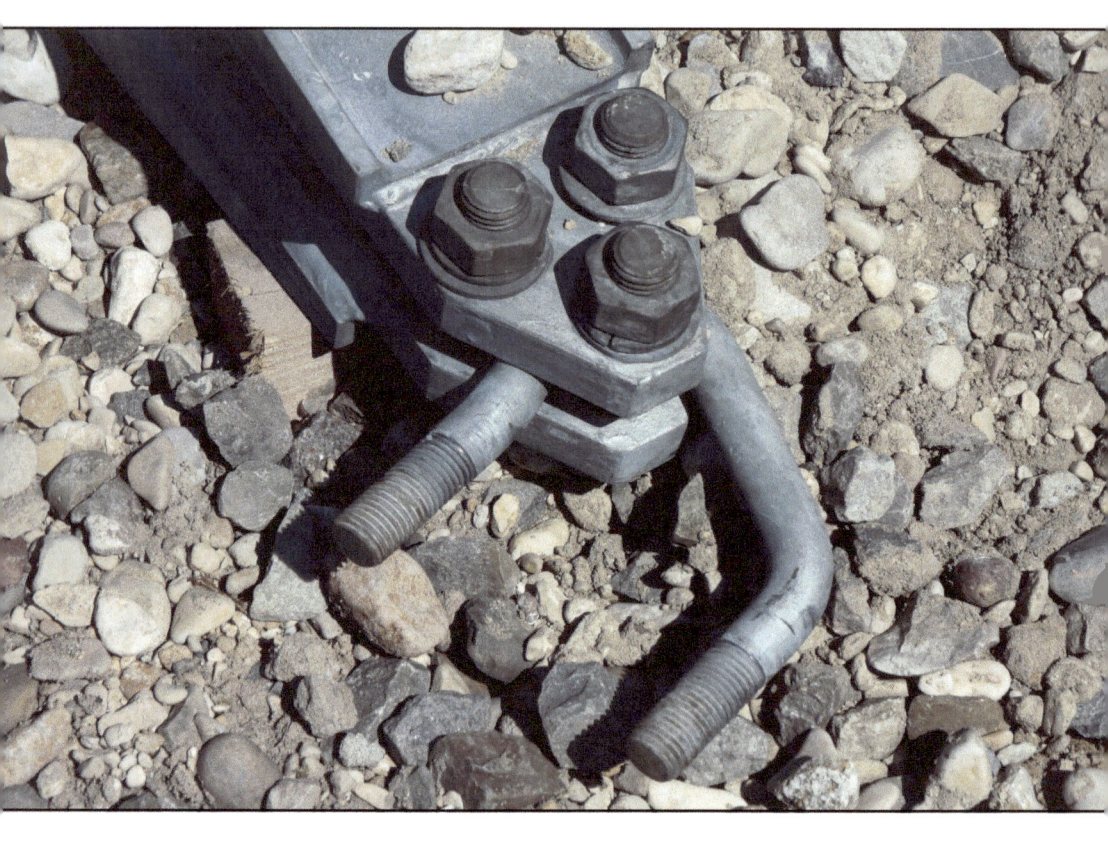

"What is it?"

Lat didn't reply at first.

"Look," Lat said, "this isn't much. Especially compared to all the destruction around here. It's only ten grams."

"You've got the best instincts of anybody I know." J-rex said. "What is it?"

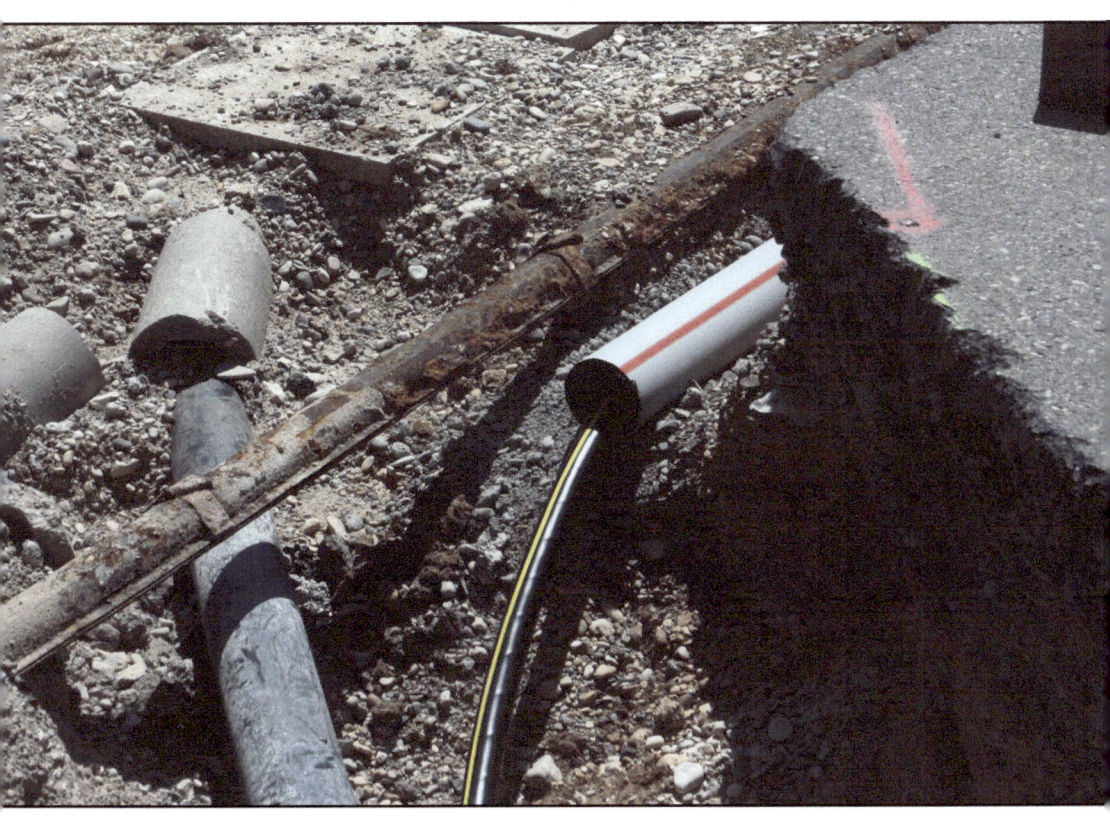

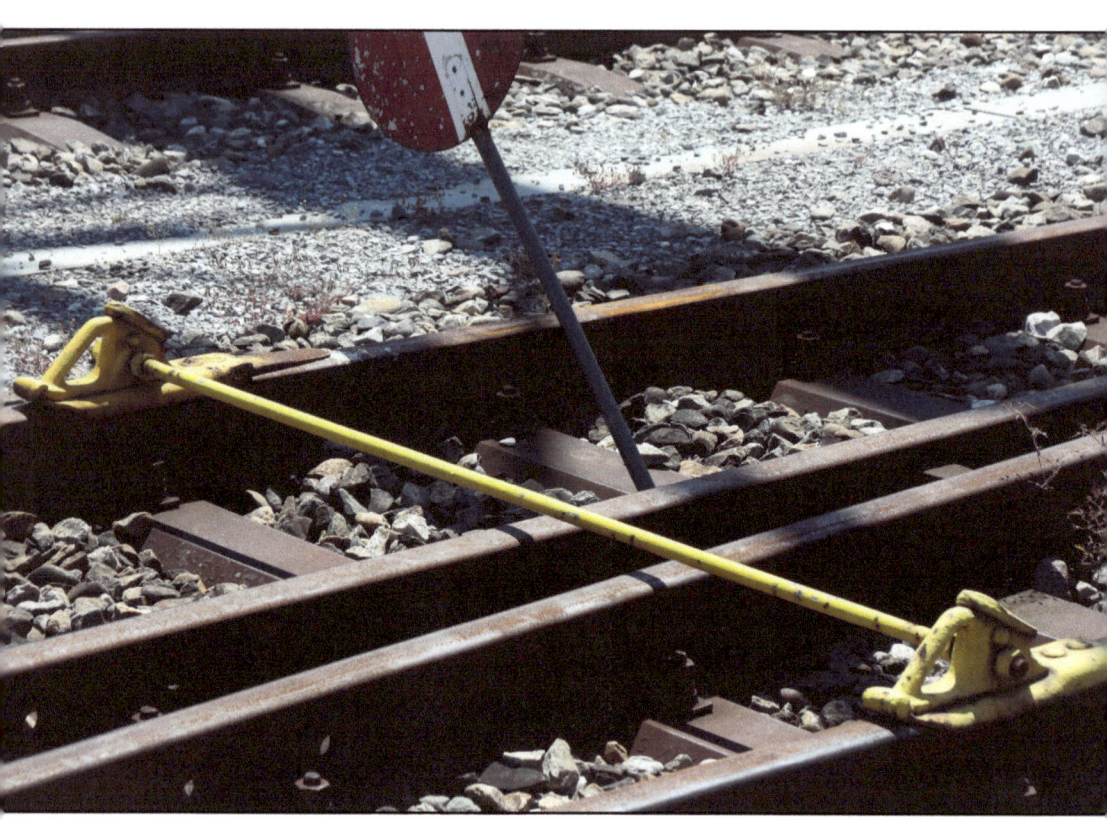

"You've got plenty to worry about with the gator," Lat said. "But you'd better recall MediCorp Team Two, just to be safe."

"*Everybody* has been recalled."

"Fine. But the only people I care about right now are those in MediCorp Team Two. And that gator better not smash up your Decontamination Chamber, because I need it to run some tests on Team Two when they get back."

"We were here so long, this may be nothing. But if the gator that smashed the lab is the same gator that we thought was dead for three days of exams. . . ."

Lat didn't finish the sentence.

"What's the worst case?" J-rex asked.

"Several of the gator's organs were liquified." Lat hesitated. "I think. . . ." Then he blurted it out. Right or wrong, this was no time for caution. "I think maybe someone on Team Two has organs that are liquifying. I think there's someone on Team Two who's infected with whatever this gator has. Someone who right now is mixing with the general population."

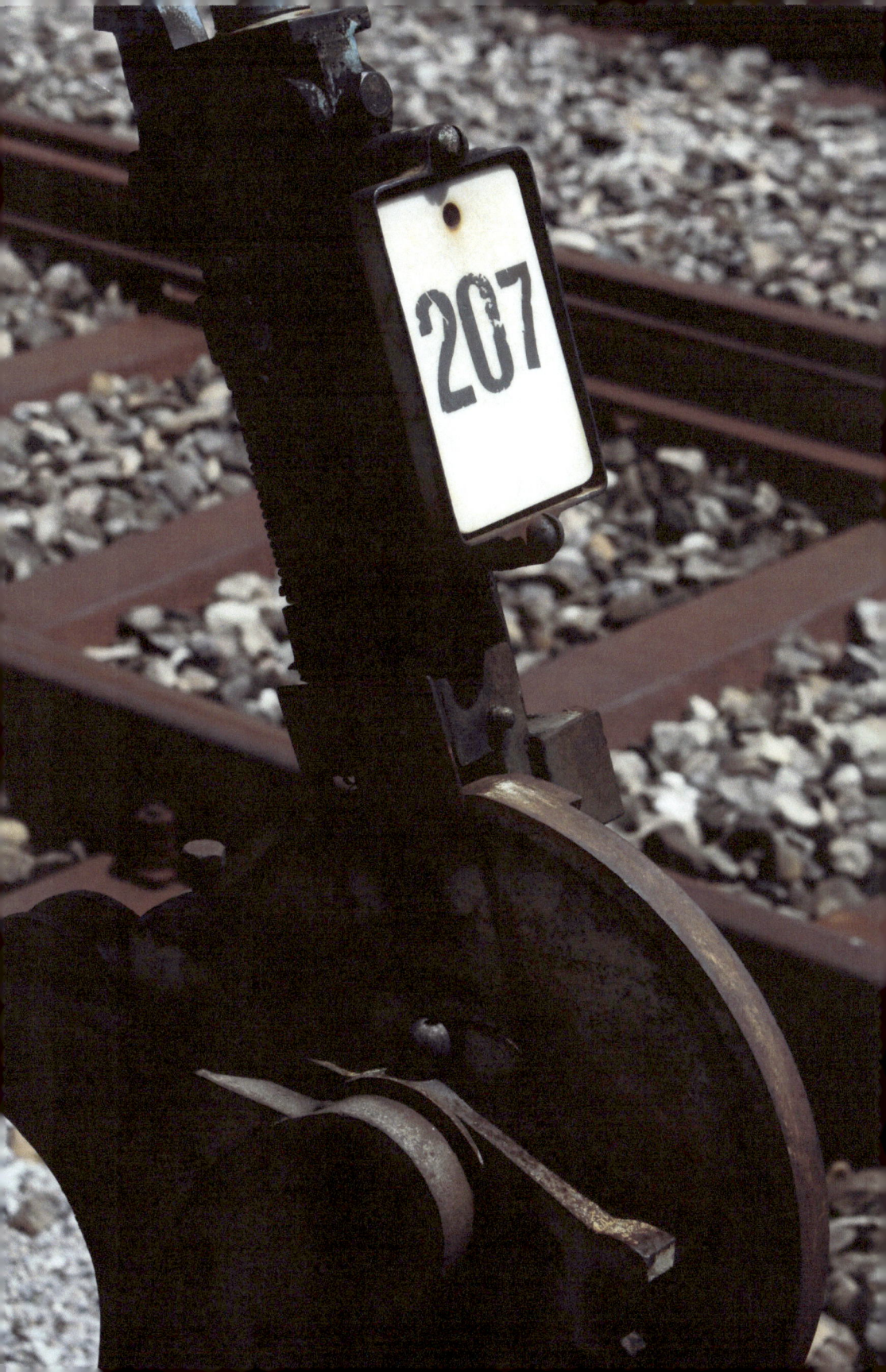

Lat paused. "J-rex, I don't want to die today. But if you get Team Two back here and you don't go to ten or eleven, you're an idiot."

J-rex let it slide. Normally, nobody ever talked to him like that and got away with it. But in this case, he thought Lat was probably right.

~~

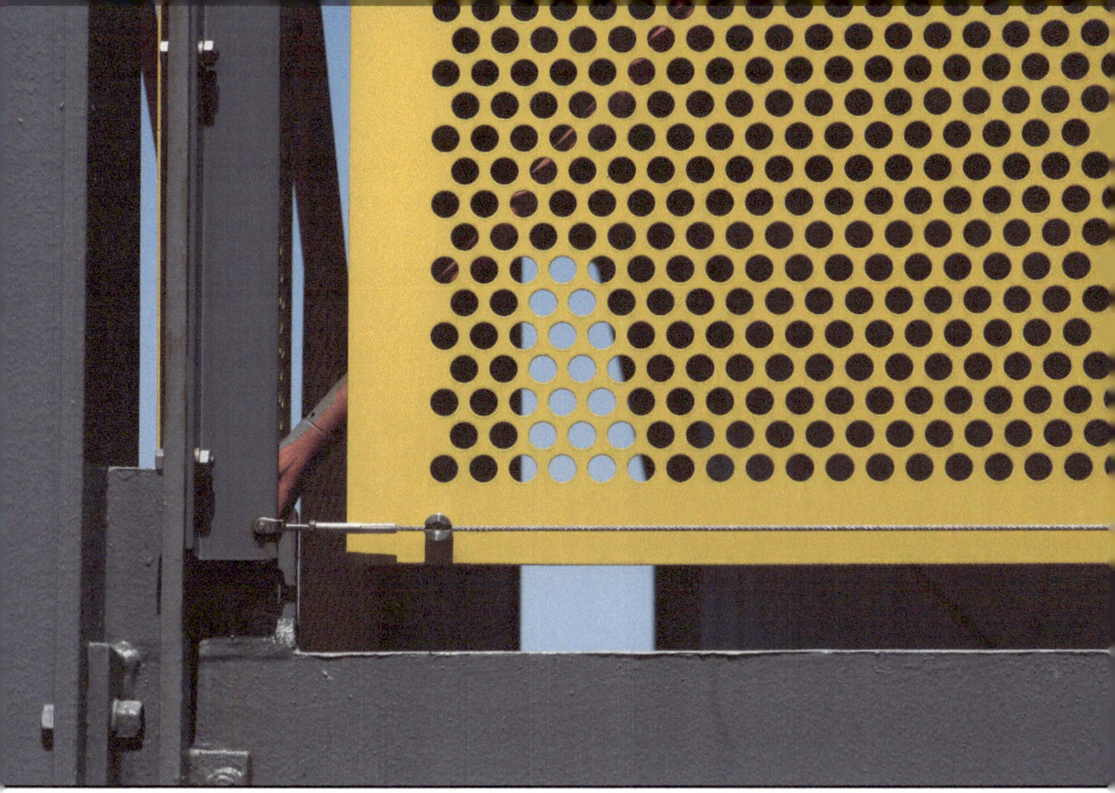

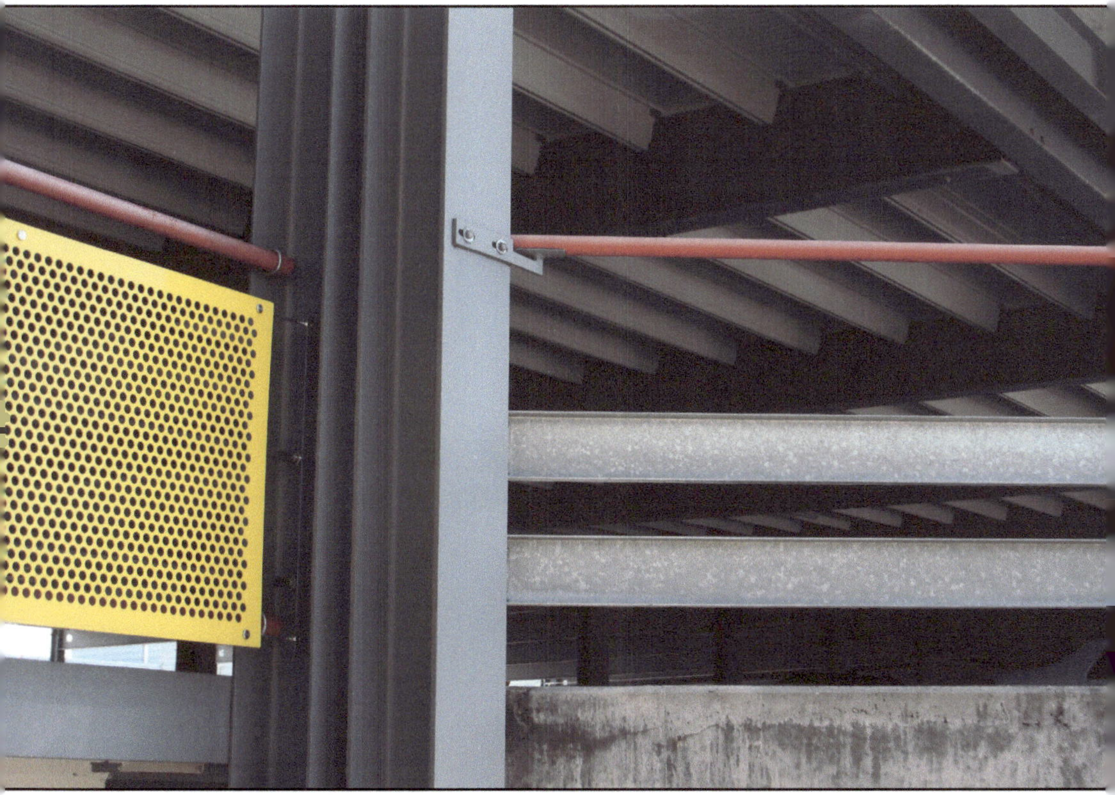

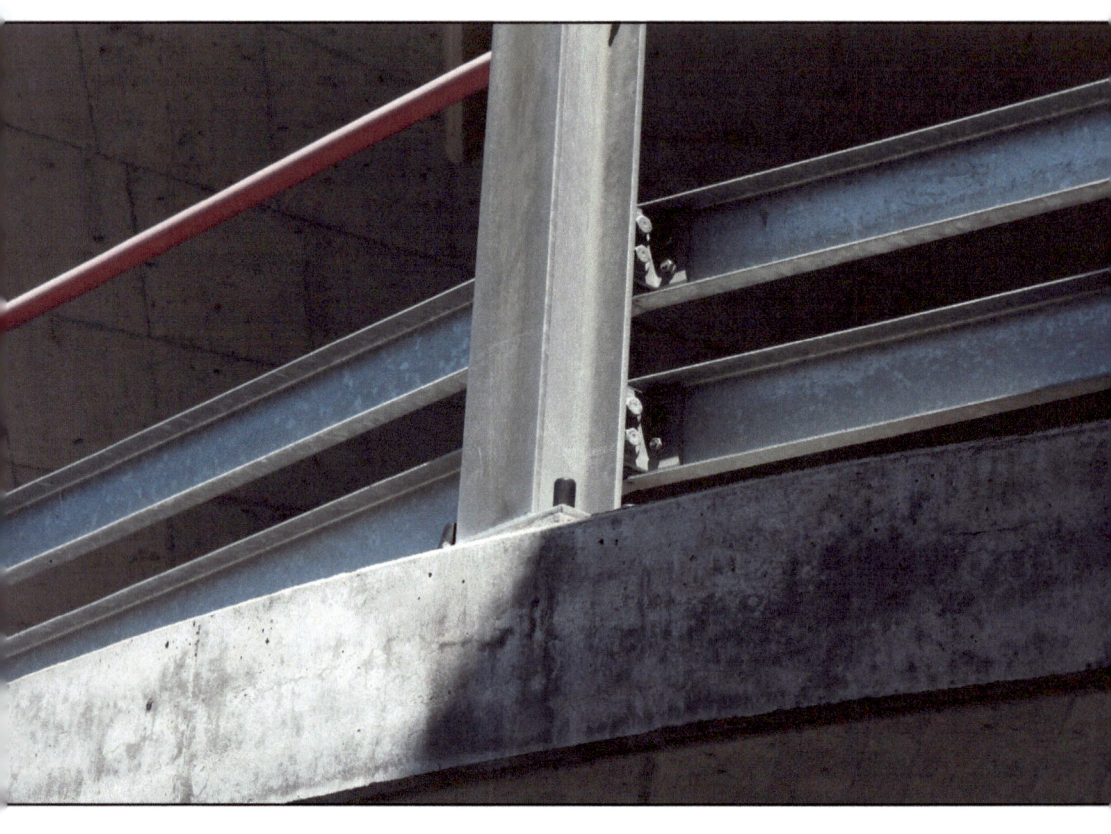

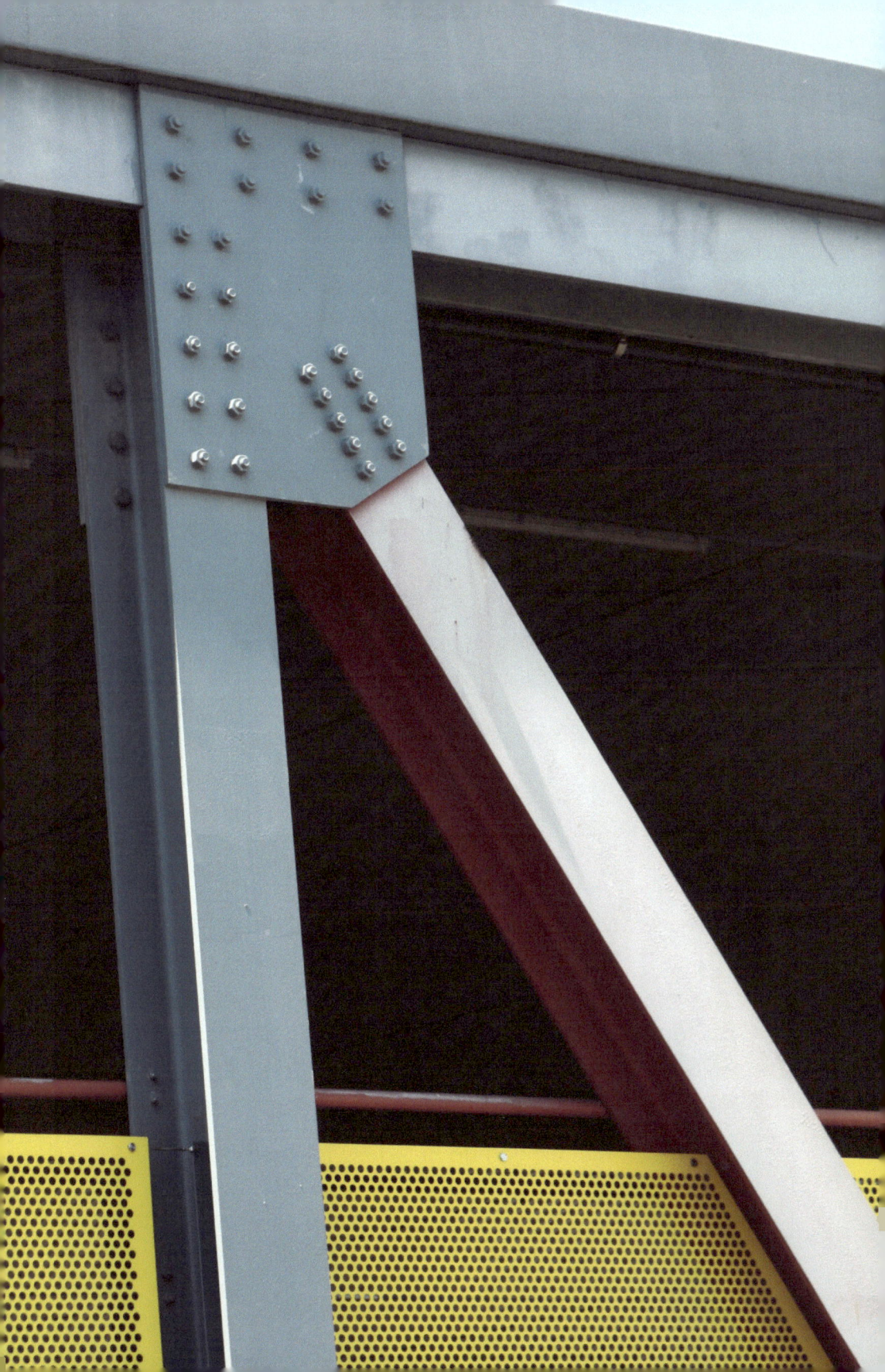

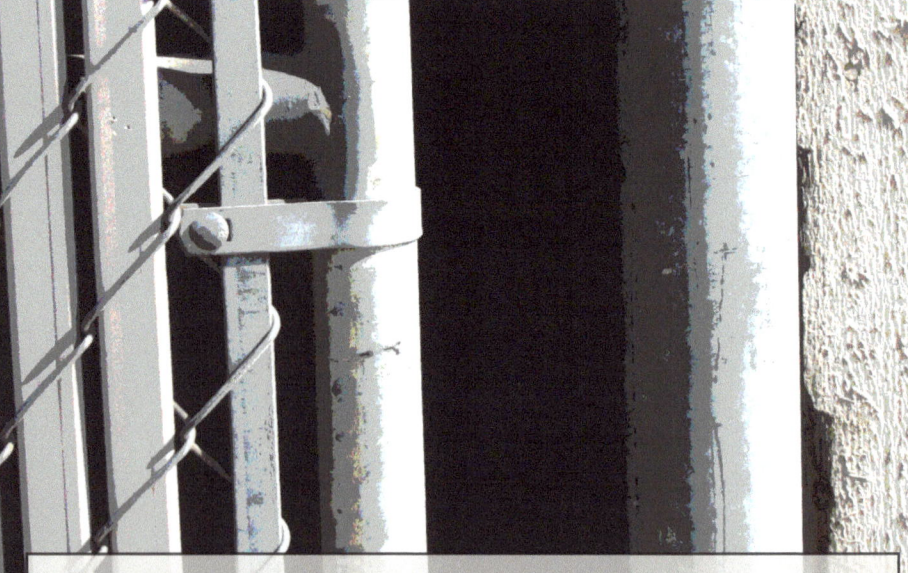

A Mark Dahle Portfolio

Derrack's Folly

Present Divestment #5

This Mark Dahle Portfolio includes a colorful abstract painting, twenty-six slightly altered photographs, and a story about a mom trying to stay calm in an emergency.

Lisa smiled and relaxed. In five minutes she'd be at the school picking up her kids. This was going to be easy.

A Mark Dahle Portfolio

Escape

Present Divestment #6

This Mark Dahle Portfolio includes a colorful abstract painting, twenty-five gorgeous photographs from Florida, and a story about a family trying to escape disaster.

Lisa pulled down her jacket and walked briskly into the entrance to the employment office. Earlier she had thought it would be easy to pick up her kids. Now she wondered if she had any chance at all to get her son. She had too much experience already with the Feast.

A Mark Dahle Portfolio

Anomalies

Present Divestment #7

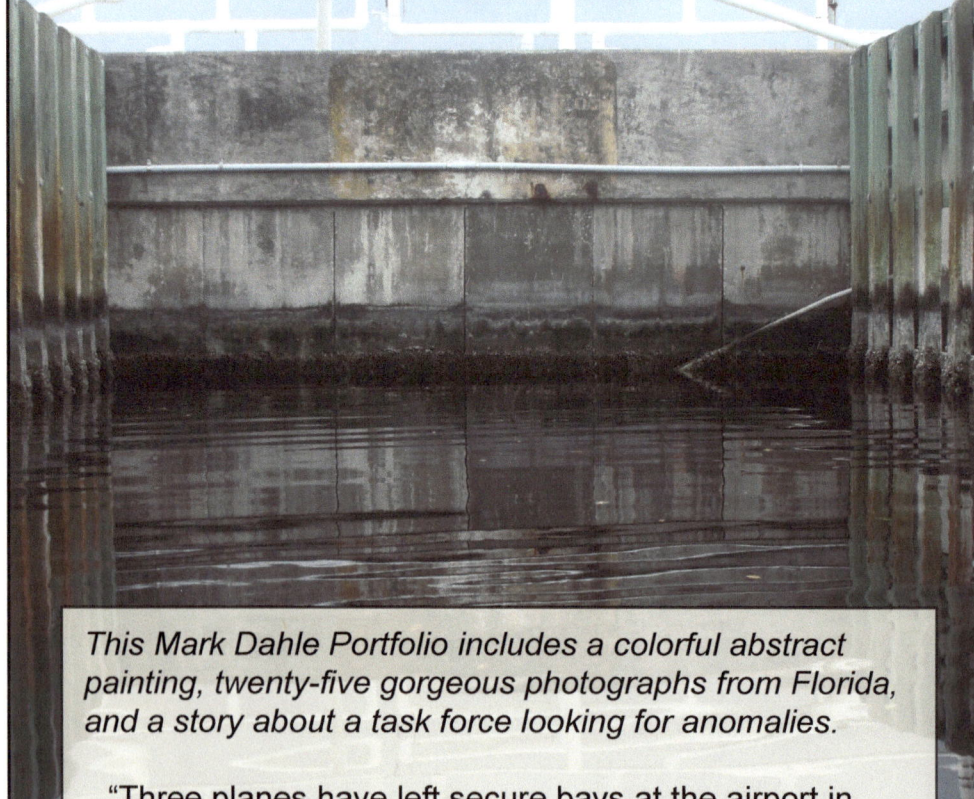

This Mark Dahle Portfolio includes a colorful abstract painting, twenty-five gorgeous photographs from Florida, and a story about a task force looking for anomalies.

"Three planes have left secure bays at the airport in the past hour. Is there something I should know, sir?"

"I got a tip. I'm not sure the Corporation is really at level three. What anomalies have you seen today?"